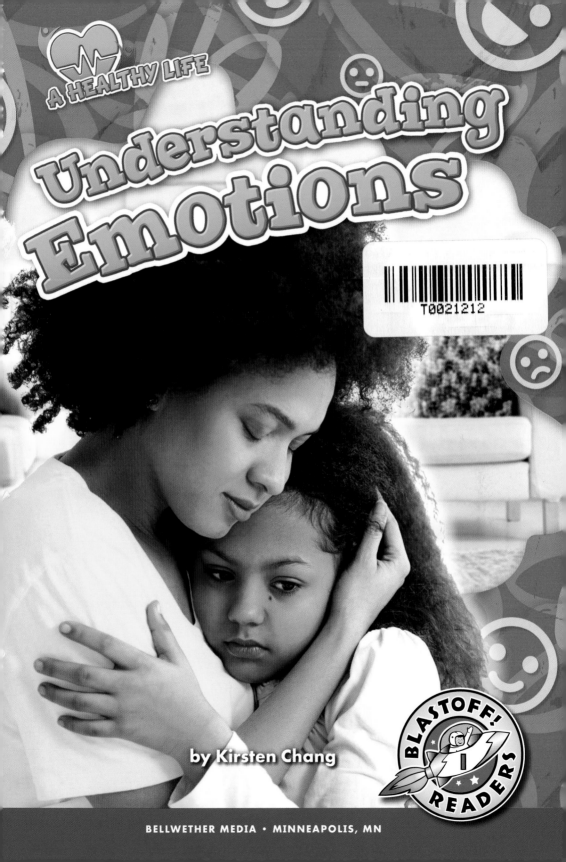

A HEALTHY LIFE

Understanding Emotions

T0021212

by Kirsten Chang

BLASTOFF! READERS

BELLWETHER MEDIA • MINNEAPOLIS, MN

Blastoff! Readers are carefully developed by literacy experts to build reading stamina and move students toward fluency by combining standards-based content with developmentally appropriate text.

Level 1 provides the most support through repetition of high-frequency words, light text, predictable sentence patterns, and strong visual support.

Level 2 offers early readers a bit more challenge through varied sentences, increased text load, and text-supportive special features.

Level 3 advances early-fluent readers toward fluency through increased text load, less reliance on photos, advancing concepts, longer sentences, and more complex special features.

★ **Blastoff! Universe**

Reading Level

Grade **K**

Grades **1–3**

Grade **4**

This edition first published in 2022 by Bellwether Media, Inc.

No part of this publication may be reproduced in whole or in part without written permission of the publisher. For information regarding permission, write to Bellwether Media, Inc., Attention: Permissions Department, 6012 Blue Circle Drive, Minnetonka, MN 55343.

Library of Congress Cataloging-in-Publication Data

Names: Chang, Kirsten, 1991- author.
Title: Understanding emotions / by Kirsten Chang.
Description: Minneapolis, MN : Bellwether Media, 2022. | Series: A healthy life | Includes bibliographical references and index. | Audience: Ages 5-8 | Audience: Grades K-1 | Summary: "Developed by literacy experts for students in kindergarten through grade three, this book introduces the importance of understanding emotions to young readers through leveled text and related photos"– Provided by publisher.
Identifiers: LCCN 2021041250 (print) | LCCN 2021041251 (ebook) | ISBN 9781644875827 (library binding) | ISBN 9781648346675 (paperback) | ISBN 9781648345937 (ebook)
Subjects: LCSH: Emotions–Juvenile literature. | Emotions in children–Juvenile literature.
Classification: LCC BF723.E6 C43 2022 (print) | LCC BF723.E6 (ebook) | DDC 152.4–dc23
LC record available at https://lccn.loc.gov/2021041250
LC ebook record available at https://lccn.loc.gov/2021041251

Editor: Rebecca Sabelko   Designer: Andrea Schneider

Printed in the United States of America, North Mankato, MN.

Table of Contents

Lia lost the game. She feels upset. She takes deep breaths. She feels better.

Why Is Understanding Emotions Important?

Understanding emotions helps us have better **mental health**.

Things do not always go well. Understanding emotions helps us **cope** with problems.

Understanding emotions helps us feel good about ourselves.

It gives us **empathy**.
We get along better
with others.

How Does Understanding Emotions Help?

better mental health

cope with problems

feel empathy

13

We may hurt others when we do not understand emotions. We may hit or yell.

How Do We Understand Emotions?

We can name our feelings. This helps us understand how we feel.

Maya is angry.
Andy took her toy.
She counts to 10.
She asks for it back.

Tools for Understanding Emotions

deep breaths

name emotions

talk to trusted adults

AJ talks to her parents. Now she understands her feelings!

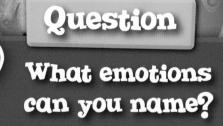

Question

What emotions
can you name?

Glossary

cope

to succeed in dealing with a hard problem

mental health

the state of how we think, feel, and act

empathy

the understanding of other people's feelings

To Learn More

AT THE LIBRARY

Culliford, Amy. *Angry*. New York, N.Y.:
Crabtree Publishing, 2021.

Devera, Czeena. *Sadness*. Ann Arbor, Mich.:
Cherry Lake Publishing, 2021.

Jaycox, Jaclyn. *Sometimes I Feel Excited*.
North Mankato, Minn.: Pebble, 2022.

ON THE WEB

FACTSURFER

Factsurfer.com gives you
a safe, fun way to find
more information.

1. Go to www.factsurfer.com.

2. Enter "understanding emotions"
   into the search box and click 🔍.

3. Select your book cover to see
   a list of related content.

Index